A New Revolution

Kevin T. Eye

Dedicated to the inextinguishable spirit of the American people and to all those who fight every day to keep the flame of freedom ablaze.

"Hook me up a new revolution, 'cause this one is a lie. We sat around laughing and watched the last one die." *Learn to Fly*, Foo Fighters, American Rock Band, 1999

In the year of our Lord 2016, our anxious nation finds itself at a crossroads, knowing that this year will be one that forever shapes the future of America. I believe without a shred of doubt that generations to come will revere 2016 in much the same way we do today with the watershed moments of 1776 and 1941. These were the years in which the brave actions of citizens, patriots and soldiers sheltered liberty, freedom and hope from evil. These were the rarest of moments in history, ones that forever changed the course of our nation and with it the fortunes of the entire world. And now, just as it was in those seminal years, the fate of America itself hangs in the balance again, forevermore to be affected by the choices made in a single momentous year.

Today, we can either fundamentally change America or we can fundamentally change America. This is not accidental redundancy; these are two very distinct choices and the final product of either action will define the American experiment forever.

There is a clear choice in this election year. We can choose to continue down the path of forced social integration, timid leadership, political correctness, government dependency, crippling debt and bleeding heart progressivism. This path involves reelecting the status quo and continuing the same ineffectual policies that both political parties have worked to push down the throats of every American for the past twenty-odd years.

Or we can choose a different path; one that is less definite then the current debacle, but one that holds with it the promise of a new America that mirrors the best of the old America. This path involves electing imperfect messengers born outside the grip of Washingtonian power. This uprising against the established is spearheaded by a few anti-Washington politicians and by one unique non-politician who is light on policy specifics, but abounding with divisive yet majestic visions that are in direct conflict to the policies of professional power brokers. Any non-traditional politician holds a certain degree of risk, but there is no reward to be had without assuming risk. We are unfortunately at the point in history where such exceptional action must be taken to have any prayer of passing a free nation onto our children and those generations to come.

It is not my intention to disparage any one particular political entity or for that matter any specific politician. Ultimately, the legacy and good name of political leaders will not be determined by wealthy endowers, media pundits or celebrity accolades. Their deeds will instead be judged by the Creator. I am but a simple man; a nurse by trade, a husband by the wonderful hand of fate and a father by the grace of God. I have a college degree, but I am by no means a political expert or a philosophical heavyweight. More appropriately, I am a simple barstool psychologist. I sense the joys and pains and the hopes and the fears of fellow Americans through the dim lights of flat screen TVs hung above the bar and in between the frosty glasses of beer and shaken not stirred martinis. My political opinion is shaped by the patrons of the taverns, the worshipers of the churches, by the words of those men and women that drive the highways of America and work tirelessly just to make due, by the words of our Founding Fathers and by my own deep rooted belief that political party identification is subservient to principal, liberty, human rights, honesty, God and the idea of American greatness.

So that really doesn't make me either a Democrat or Republican. Because neither of these political entities believe that they are subservient to anything. They have left their faithful service to the public in the wake of blind greed funded by their shortsighted political cronies and the Washington lobbyists. Their honor has been dismantled by a persistent and vile dishonesty to the voters. Finally, they have completely buried their morals under a mountain of deliberate actions that have made many of them treasonous to a nation that some of us still hold dear.

These detached minions of both political parties are now fueled by an inexhaustible need to remain in power. It is no longer born from a desire to serve the public or out of a duty to country. It is now carefully cultivated, almost genetically engineered, by unrelated and often unelected vermin entrenched in a system so broken and corrupted that we no longer remember a time when it wasn't broken or corrupted . Mr. Smith no longer goes to Washington. He is selected, scrubbed, intimidated, force fed talking points, indebted, and regurgitated every two, four or six years by an amalgamation of corporations, image consultants, financiers, party elite and by other figures that we wouldn't trust to walk our dog. The end result of decades of stacking the political system with such well-coifed drones has led directly to the miserable state of affairs that every Democrat, Republican, Independent or breathing individual of this nation faces today.

The greater good that once was a guiding principle is now neither greater or good. Policy is formulated to enrich the well-connected without regard to the needs of the many. For those poor souls, the masses that have been left behind by countless elected officials, the government can only muster the meager energy to dangle a carrot in front of them. Our representatives disingenuously promise the possibility of a better future, one that almost certainly involves more suckling to Mother Government, while simultaneously providing for a dependent and despondent present. Year after year, empty suits and empty skirts promise economic relief and opportunity to the poor huddled masses. They stand at the podium and spew forth teleprompter-fed threats that a vote for those on the other side leads to Armageddon. They propagandize the belief that their opposition is evil incarnate; they will come and take away your housing, your food, your health care, your ObamaPhone and your right to choose. And somehow, these buffoons are reelected and will rehash the same tired rhetoric next time around. And the next time around. And the next time around, and by the next time, these serial liars are now holding court with the exact same people from previous elections, now forlornly standing beside their children and their grandchildren, all still dependent and downcast, and still afraid that someone will cruelly take it away and leave them with less than the very little they still have. By this point, they have forever lost sight of the carrot. They no longer even care about the carrot.

Truth be known, the other side wouldn't take it all away anyway. It is much too convenient nowadays to placate the poor with just enough to keep them hooked. Republicans that promise welfare reform are about as genuine as a Rolex from a street vendor on Times Square. It looks good from a distance and is right twice a day. Upon closer examination it is a piece of flimsy tin that is useless and falls apart within a week. The stump speeches promising tax relief and entitlement reforms are simply click bait, aimed directly at those that foot the bill and are tired of continually doing so. It gives the vague appearance of a contrast with the free-spending, government-is-the-answer Democrats, but it really is all for show.

In fact, most of all the supposed contrasts between the current rotten crop of Democrats and Republicans is less Hatfield and McCoy and more like *Laverne and Shirley*. They publically squabble over budgets and abortion rights, and they jab at each other over entitlements and foreign policy, and they occasionally insult the supposed intellect of the other side. In the end though, little is ever really changed. Washington either exists in a state of perpetual gridlock, or it produces some form of legislation that is guaranteed to screw over the vast majority of the population. And it is done with the full cooperation of both sides of the political spectrum.

I used to think that such subterranean cooperation was stuff of conspiracy theory. In order to speak of such nonsense you needed to be living in your mother's basement and you needed to own at least three tin foil hats of varying size. The past few months though have revealed a disturbance in the Force, a gradual but obvious unraveling of the very things that were woven right in front of our blind eyes all along. We are only now starting to dissect those unholy partnerships that were made long ago with our unintentional cooperation. What was once two sides of the aisle, two distinctly different political parties and three equal branches of government have morphed into one ominous sentinel. Those divergent forces have now become singular in body and purpose with the explicit goal of maintaining their status quo at any cost.

Our Founding Fathers were smart enough to envision such treachery and did their best to ensure the Republic would endure for centuries by prohibiting such a monster from being born. They created two spectacular documents, the Constitution and the Bill of Rights, that provided the guide for how government was to function in a brave new world. The government they envisioned would be a participatory government, one in which the people had equal representation and voice. They saw a distinct separation of State and Federal powers. Fearful of monarchial rule, they ensured there were ample checks and balances at the national level so no one entity would wield more power than the other. They stressed the absolute need for individual rights going as far as to spelling them out and they believed these rights should be protected above all others. They understood that in order to form a more perfect Union, the rights of individuals must always supersede those of the government. They knew that society would progress forward and allowed for us to be smarter tomorrow than today through a formal amendment process. It was through that superb process that slavery was abolished and the right to vote was guaranteed to *all* Americans. The Founders envisioned a dynamic government with robust legislative and electorate debate, fair and equal application of laws, an apolitical high court that ruled solely on the Constitutionality of laws, a system that allowed states to govern themselves on local matters and they envisioned an engaged electorate willing to hold each and every government representative accountable.

For the better part of 200 years, it worked and worked beautifully. The evidence was there. No country could remotely match what the United States of America once was. Countries marveled at our ingenuity, individual freedoms, opportunities, wealth and global influence. Many countries copied our Constitution as the blueprint for their own. Our original revolution ignited a global revolution where kings and queens feared the population and ceded ever-increasing powers and authority to the people. In times of great global distress, the entire world looked to America for proof that democracy and decency would prevail over dictators and oppression. It was a remarkable run.

The Founding Fathers simply couldn't envision the massive scale of the abject corruption to come. They couldn't envision super PACs and would never believe the level of influence the mighty few have over the whole legislature. They couldn't see a country that would spend itself into oblivion to wage useless wars, to enslave the poor with entitlements, to rescue banks and corporations from their own greed and to fritter the people's money away on pork projects and government waste. There was absolutely no way that our Founders could perceive that the government they fought to create would someday conspire to promote a population so numb to the political process; so detached from it, so repulsed by it, and so bitterly divided, that in the fog of disenfranchisement the government itself would grab the power meant for the people.

The Founding Fathers were good. They were damn good, but they never would recognize this America.

Along the way, both political parties figured out that to achieve the end goal; whatever that end goal is, they would need to consolidate the power and systemically disassemble the American Republic. I am not remotely smart enough to understand or decipher what the Establishment's ultimate motive is. Some say the end game is to have complete control over the population. Some believe that it involves a new world order bent on global enslavement. All I know is that it doesn't involve a return to Constitutional principles or expansion of personal freedom or anything remotely on those lines. It involves something to the exact contrary and that is very frightening. I can barely remember an America that was noble and prosperous. I can barely remember an America led by men of substance and conviction and determination. I still have faded visions of a country that was led by people with at least a modicum of desire for the greater good. I feel pity for the generations after me, generations that have never seen even a glimpse of America at its best. There are so many among us that actually believe that today is the pinnacle of America's greatness. They are unfortunately lost in not recognizing the zenith occurred long ago. What we have today are remote vestiges of a better time and for those younger than me, they never really had a chance to remotely appreciate what has been stolen from us by the leviathan government.

Some revolutions occur overnight and some revolutions take generations. Some are accomplished by the bullet and some are done in peace by the sheer will of millions. Yet some revolutions are quietly and insidiously conscripted from within. If the second American revolution was going to be televised, it was not going to be a live event.

It was going to be carefully scripted and systemically implemented point by point.

It all started with controlling the message because that is a most significant component when controlling the masses. The government needed to ensure the cooperation of the electronic media outlets as well as the print publications and the mainstream media. All were eventually enticed to be compliant, a concubine to the government masters . News organizations began to lean heavily toward the left, so dubbed the Liberal Media. In essence though, which way national media players leaned was really not important. Liberals always had a more palatable and digestible message to sell. That is why the youth is so attracted to it before they become old, bitter and gainfully employed. On the surface, the ideas that Liberals promoted were simply more show worthy, more easily consumed by a public that desired image over message and flair over substance. With the help of hack

Hollywood script writers and actors and actresses with liposuction-enhanced six-pack abs and airbrushed smiles, the manifesto was subjected to rewrites, given as many retakes as necessary, etched in celluloid and digitized for your viewing pleasure The visions of government-sponsored hope and blended families and rage against the rich old guardians of evil, set to the soundtrack of our lives, was a far prettier girl than whatever the Conservative proponents could muster. It was the path of least resistance that pulled the media to the left.

At issue was the fact that media *chose sides* and they were never supposed to do so; the freedom of the press was hijacked to promote carefully-crafted messages. Network producers ensured that the truth was rarely televised and whenever it was, it was done purposely to discredit, destroy, disengage or depress any given target audience. Dissenting opinions were quickly silenced, and those few that dared to disagree were branded as heretics or racists or bigots or incompetent.   Gone was the straight-forward trustworthiness of icons such as Walter Cronkite. They were replaced by talking pinheads like Brian Williams and Katie Couric, people with about as much substance as a cone of cotton candy. The government accomplished this coup much in the same way they accomplished every insidious move against the American public. They simply instituted some regulatory alphabet agency to enforce rules (FCC) and threatened the networks with additional sanctions or regulations. This became the tried and true playbook going forward to control whatever entity that seemed beyond their blood-sucking tentacles. They got in bed with the CEO's and the board members and showed them the incredible profitability that existed within the corrupted message. They then threw in a dash of threatened access restriction and threats of never-ending litigation and the mainstream media soon realized the battle against was not worth risking the fortune that was ahead.

The government didn't just stop at the news though, they pushed even further to control the content of the regularly-scheduled programming itself. Content went from faith and family based programming to mindless eye candy designed to distract and shock but never to enlighten or inspire. Gone was *Little House on the Prairie*, replaced by *Bachelor Pad*. Gone was *Highway to Heaven*, replaced by *Road Rules*. Gone was *Touched by an Angel*, replaced by *Touched by a Kardashian* or something of that ilk. Traditional relationships were shown to be so 1980s. The new relationship model was to take 20 strangers and have them all compete against each other for the affection of one universally attractive member of the opposite sex. Love was not shown to be something special or everlasting but instead it was shown as superficial, physical, unimportantly spread between multiple choices, and forged over the course of a television season for all to see. The story of classic romance was gone and there would not be any happily ever after moments shown. Instead, Lifetime Network movies of women wronged and seeking vengeance flickered across the cable lines and satellite signals. On the rare occasions when any remotely wholesome programming was shown, the ratings were good but networks deemed the target audience to be too old or undesirable. Demographics ruled the programming decisions with direction from the government above. The message finally had a powerful medium for mass dissemination.

Then the internet exploded and the Silicon Valley elite played along too, becoming billionaires themselves along the way. Website after website popped up and populated the message in 140 characters or less, on our smart phones and tablets and on our computer monitors. Local newspapers, often the last vestige of true investigative journalism, cut staff and reduced printings under the weight of declining revenues. The information superhighway was hijacked and new diversions were presented to an ever-distracted population. Whatever message that needed pushed to the populace could be done so at light speed, everywhere, in every corner of the country, on every platform, infecting every mind. Is there any wonder that it is called "going viral?"

It was all carefully crafted. Do you really think a bunch of network executives spontaneously sat down one day and said "Hey, I bet people would just *love* to watch a show about the hard decisions that a female Secretary of State has to make. Let's call it *Madam Secretary*?" That isn't art imitating life is it?

There might be some remnants of faith-based programming still on TV, although I suspect it is probably sandwiched somewhere between the ass cheeks of any given Kardashian on a Saturday night where no one will watch.

Next on the list was the battle for the hearts and minds of the American youth. To ensure future generations were primed to accept the message, the government interjected itself profoundly into the classrooms and textbooks and lunchrooms across the land. Curriculums were shaped to standardize education; ensuring that all children received the same teaching leading to the same message. History was deemphasized and revised. America's past accomplishments were downplayed and America's faults were brought to the forefront. Teaching to the test became the norm as another formal way to ensure compliance with a rigid teaching agenda. The *Pledge of Allegiance* was removed from the daily morning routine for fear that some 8 year old atheist might become offended by "One Nation Under God." The mention of anything related to religion, especially Judeo-Christian beliefs, was strictly forbidden. The government was able to achieve compliance through regulatory statutes that helped to neuter the local control of the schools and through the usual threats of funding removal. Children were sufficiently molded and they left the school systems with little appreciation or pride for what was once American greatness. They left the school system cynical of their future and programmed with a powerful message that government was always the answer to any question.

This of course led an ever-increasing number to become dependent on that government. The political machine simply played along and encouraged the increase in the welfare rolls and then proceeded to tighten the grip through the aptly misnamed Affordable Care Act. A person's health care was controlled by the Federal overlords. No real efforts were made to change the stars of those oppressed. Those in power casted the blame for society's ills upon the successful and not on their own failed policies that were planned for failure from inception. Various ideas of distribution of wealth were floated to placate the cries for more subsidy. The government used its alphabet agencies such as the EPA and the IRS to tax, fine, or impose sanctions on any business, individual or advocate for the sensible that opposed its rapidly expanding social agenda. Those citizens that participated in the Federal programs did not see any appreciable improvement in their quality of life, but they continued to feel trapped and were unable to compete against cheaper imported labor and in a dwindling job market. The cycle of poverty was continued. Whenever the government was not able to actually own a private industry, excessive regulation and control was placed on the business to ensure that the entity will follow the government's wishes. Large portions of the population no longer were employed and private industry became fearful of more regulation and government involvement. These industries were increasingly reluctant to invest further in a nation in obvious decline and they looked elsewhere to invest their ever-increasing profits.

Just controlling the media, the population and the education system was still not enough. The sovereignty of the nation itself was placed in peril. Trade agreements were made to placate selected big businesses and this encouraged the off shoring of jobs and manufacturing. Markets that were supposed to be open to American business remained largely closed. The remaining domestic manufacturing base withered under the weight of manipulated foreign currencies and cheap dumped goods. To expand an ever-shrinking world market, efforts were made to open up markets in hostile territories such as Iran and Cuba, countries controlled by murderous dictators with a deep-seeded hatred for America. Where so possible, the government involved itself to the greatest extent possible in all aspects of commerce and business. Allowances were made for business to seek corporate inversions, effectively encouraging American-based businesses to move their corporate headquarters to a foreign country to avoid corporate taxes. Massive sums of profits were then held by companies outside the USA, and no real effort was made to recoup the stashed cash. Greater burdens were placed on existing businesses and working individuals. Businesses threatened to leave municipalities or America altogether unless tax relief was given. The sadistic cycle of corporate welfare was put in play, leaving individual taxpayers footing the ballooning bill. Government spending increased exponentially while revenue remained flat. The nation's deficit threatened social programs that helped to provide a safety net for the aged and frail. Those people, the ones that toiled in the factories, raised the next generation, fought on foreign lands, fed the nation and built the infrastructure that everyone took for granted, were promised care to the grave. They paid their dues and taxes in spades. Instead of living out their golden years in relative security, many held to the sad hope that they would die before their health benefits, pensions or Social Security evaporated.

It wasn't long before the conspirators realized that not every job can be off shored. To alleviate this problem, the government employed a tactic of lax border protection, allowing over 14 million illegal immigrants into the country. Law enforcement agencies were told purposely stand down and not to deport those breaking the law. After failing to change the laws that would have given amnesty to people that have purposely and repeatedly broken multiple federal laws, executive actions not authorized in the Constitution were dictated to add the necessary legitimacy to legal inaction. Illegal aliens became illegal immigrants then became undocumented immigrants in media circles to accentuate a positive message set forth by the government. Many of the immigrants had children that became American citizens. The term "anchor baby" was reviled in the mainstream media, yet no concise term was popularized to define a child that was born in America for the singular purpose of preventing the mother and other family members from being deported. The 14 million plus illegal humans were given benefits and monies from the Federal government. They were given jobs at depressed wages by the corporate entities. Neither political party had the will to address the issue in any comprehensive manner and both parties deftly danced around any meaningful legislation aimed stopping more immigrants from flooding into America. In fact, a Herculean effort was made by many in the legislature to actually legalize the millions, but the attempt is ultimately defeated due unexpected overwhelming pressure from voters and the staunch actions of the few all-too-rare patriots left in Congress . Despite overwhelming public opposition to a path to citizenship and overwhelming support for border control, nothing was enforced and nothing was done. American-born citizens continued to struggle to find employment in the face of the massive cheap illegal labor pool. Additional people requiring government assistance further burdened local agencies and added to a ballooning national debt. Sanctuary cities were founded and funded to provide safe haven for illegal immigrants, even for those that have committed multiple violent crimes against American citizens. Public opinion was profoundly shaped by the Establishment to accept the immigrants, and those that openly opposed illegal immigration are branded as Nationalists, right-wing nut jobs, Fascists or worse.

Any legislative impairments to the grand scheme had to be removed as well. To work around those few stragglers in Congress that still believed in the Constitution, the President signed multiple executive actions that circumvent Congressional authority. Publically, the Congress squawked and threatened legislative and legal action, but this public display of fake admonishment had the effect of a toothless man eating beef jerky. Congress itself then devised an ingenious way to deal with potential opposition to damaging legislation and unhinged deficit spending. Bills were carefully crafted behind closed doors by faithful party elitists and their benevolent benefactors, hidden from the light of the public and from the challenges of those that would dare to initiate vigorous debate. The pending legislations were then unleashed on the Congressional body mere hours before voting, making it impossible to read the legislation or to even discuss what damage the actions will do the American public. And in the rare instances when good sense seemed to triumph, the Supreme Court was called upon legislate rather than to deliberate as outlined in the increasingly irreverent Constitution.

All three branches of government were finally matched in relative synchronization. The two formally warring political parties combined into one bipolar parasite, feeding off each other and off the influence of endless money. The checks and balances envisioned by the Founding Fathers were nothing but Sunday morning talk show sound bites for the masses to consume. The one governmental entity was fully formed with a singular motive of perpetual power at its core of existence.

Those that don't learn from history are doomed to repeat it. These types of government typically operate in the darkest recesses of history. In such instances, policies doing the most damage are not decided by the masses. They are decided by a relative few, done so with moral absence but with full legal justification.

Even the most evil of men still have to have some type of twisted foundation for their heinous actions. On January 20, 1942, a small group of high-ranking individuals from all branches of government were called together for a conference at a palatial estate in the Berlin suburb of Wannsee. The invitation-only meeting was called for by Reinhard Heydric, the 37 year-old director of the Reich Main Security Office. Present at the conference were fifteen men, all of which were politicians or ethicists or military leaders or party faithful with the singular purpose of discussing the logistical and legal concerns of what was termed the "Jewish problem." Over the course of the next few hours, and in between a buffet lunch and the consumption of cognac, these fifteen men engaged in light debate over definitions and phrasing and they mulled over the mechanism by which a new legally justified protocol would be implemented. In reality, everyone knew what the outcome of the meeting would be before the first cigar was lit. Any of the participants that were openly, or tenuously, opposed to the eventual outcome were taken aside by the most powerful and persuaded to agree with the party line. Agreement was not optional; it was mandatory. Before the sun had set that day, under the explicit direction of the Reich Chancellor of Germany and with the legal justification created by the Wannsee Conference, the policy of systemic genocide of the Jewish population was put into law. Fifteen men, behind closed doors, away from public scrutiny, driven by twisted logic and corrupted by power, decided the terminal fate of six million Jewish prisoners. All before dinner was served.

I am in no way comparing the unspeakable horrors unleashed by Nazi subhuman excrement to the nefarious actions committed by our own government. Killing six million people out of sheer hatred is what real Fascists do. But in this election year where images of Nazis and Adolph Hitler and shrills of the certainty of dictatorships to come are pushed along the airwaves and internet feeds, I have found the need to take pause and inventory where we are in this moment in history. Are we a republic? Are we a democracy? Are those that seek the highest office in the land incompetent, racist, untrustworthy, short-sighted, irrational, idealistic, bigoted or Fascist?

Pick any of the above adjectives and feel free to attach a candidate to it. Either by your own free will or by the impression of the media you can probably fit a name behind each of these descriptors. It is the salacious allegation that in some way the Republican candidates, especially billionaire businessman Donald Trump, freely practice Fascism that has forced me to question what that really means and to dissect some of the hyperbole that is found abundant in the popular media.

Is it Fascist for the government to control the media and ensure their message is pushed to an unsuspecting population? Is it Fascist for the government to ensure that children are provided a mechanized system of education where the only measure of success is that of standardized testing scores. Is it Fascist for these same children to not learn about the great deeds of our forefathers but rather to be taught their shortcomings and failures? Is it Fascist to expend significantly more energy to tear down American patriotism than to promote it? Is it Fascist for the government to exert heavy handed control over private business through regulations, fines, sanctions and denial of applications? Is it Fascist to enslave generation after generation of Americans with social programs that have no end goal of promoting success but instead promote poverty and continued dependence? Is it Fascist to choose which laws to enforce and which to purposefully ignore? Is it Fascist to secretly monitor the population through omnipresent video cameras and metadata collection programs without proper warrant or just cause? Is if Fascist to circumvent the most perfect form of government ever created, one in which the power of the government is derived from the governed, for personal glory or for shadowy agendas? Is it Fascist for one person to rule by decree when the laws explicitly limit such authority? Is it Fascist to conglomerate separate branches of government, authorized by the highest law in the land to be separate so as to check each other, into one entity that rubber stamps the will of any one given person or governmental body? Is it Fascist to effectively have only one political party, known henceforth as the Establishment, and to systemically discredit anyone that opposes such an entity? Is it Fascist to steadfastly continue dangerous policies that compromise the safety of the citizenship when the great majority disagree with such policies? Is it Fascist to adopt laws that apply to the population but not to the elected? Is it Fascist to tell the population which words are forbidden to speak, which flags are forbidden to fly and which beliefs no longer fit the politically correct narrative?

Or is it Fascist to say that we are going to close our boarders, remove the persons that are here illegally and deny entry into the country to those people that despise everything about America and wish to do us great harm? Is it Fascist to put America first and to adopt policies that ensure that America is equally competitive globally while still remaining a true sovereign nation? What type of people dare to breathe such fresh air? They must be "Fascists" and they must be the very the same people that cling to their guns and their religion.

Well, it is not for lack of trying by the government that we still have the right to bear arms. It remains one of the few fundamental rights that keeps the almighty government from easily controlling the population; if they so desired of course. The government has certainly become increasingly impatient in the pursuit of gun control. There was a time in America when we mourned tragedy. When mass murder happened, we bowed our heads, prayed for the families and showed reverence for the deceased. Now, partisan hacks fight to become the first to tweet how such a tragedy is yet another example of why America needs common sense gun control. The requests for prayers are sadly mocked while the requests for gun control are heartily heralded. All of this before the bodies are even cold or the blood coagulated.

Sadly, we have become this type of frigid society. We have become a nation numb to understanding the preciousness of life. We have become a nation where our leaders make sure that no good tragedy goes wasted in an effort to push their menacing agendas. We have become a society where a breach of political correctness is often worse than murder. We have become a nation where people can casually talk about the dismemberment of human fetuses while slurping wine and munching on a kale salad sprinkled with a balsamic ginger reduction dressing. We have become a society simply incapable of tapping the brakes of progress for fear that someone might just actually openly question the merits of that progress.

And what about those poor fools that cling to their religion? What about those mouth-breathers that foolishly think that divine intervention had anything to do with the miracle of founding this nation? What about those knuckle-draggers that believe that Christ is the savior and that mankind is made better through his teachings? What about those cavemen that believe life begins at conception? The Establishment's unified response: Take your inopportune religion and move on, there is nothing more to see here.

To truly control the masses, they must either be completely brainwashed or utterly demoralized. There is simply no better way strip the population of any sense of personal satisfaction than to destroy Faith.

Want to say Merry Christmas? *Screw you, someone might get offended and we strongly suggest you say happy holidays instead.* Want to say a prayer before the council meeting? *Screw you, separation of church and state.* Want to include the ENTIRE *Pledge of Allegiance* in that promo? *Screw you, we can't find the extra 0.75 seconds to include that "under God" part.* Want to have the option to not fund abortions in a health plan out of religious objection? *Screw you, it's the law.* Want to not have to fund contraception in a health plan out of religious objection? *Screw you sideways, it's the law.* Want to believe that marriage is between a man and a woman? *Screw you, it's the law, deal with it you homophobe.* Want to withhold a service provided by your privately-owned personal business out of religious objection? *Screw you, it's the law you stupid bigot.* Want to protect Christianity from those that wish to destroy it? *Screw you, we already publically apologized to the Muslim community over that silly Crusade y'all did a few hundred years ago and they are coming here to America whether you like it or not.*

Republican candidates are Fascists in disguise? Please! When an entire population is browbeaten again and again to feel ashamed about their very existence, that is not something driven by hope and change. That is something driven by hatred.

I don't have a tin foil hat. I really don't believe in conspiracy theories. I don't believe that 9/11 was an inside job. I believe it was perpetrated by Islamic extremists that simply hate our very existence. I do though believe that very little of all this is simply happenstance. Some of it has to be planned and interwoven so I will try and connect a few dots: Take a strong bloated centralized government with no accountability to itself or the voters. Add to it millions of people dependent on that government for every aspect of their life. Throw in 15 million plus immigrants under threat of deportation. Sprinkle in a steady flow of a million or so Islamic refugees that will never assimilate and who believe that our destruction is the most righteous of endeavors. Subtract a population that is disengaged, demoralized, depressed, afraid to speak freely, wrecked by political correctness and faithless. Subtract local government control and subtract an emasculated local law enforcement that is fallaciously portrayed as ineffectual and incompetent. What do you have?

Well, you still have the right to vote. Not that Mother Government hasn't done all it can do to dilute that right as well. Much to their chagrin, they fully understand that the power of the vote remains the one great equalizer and they know all too well that if ever consolidated, it can undo some of the purposeful damage. Fear not defenders of the wicked realm, the party faithful are working on destroying that too.

For example, the Democrat Party Presidential Primary allots almost 30% of the overall delegate count for the Presidential nomination to something called Super Delegates, a venue of vultures that are not bound in any way by the actual will of the voters. These unaccountable zombies represent nearly one third of the total number of delegates needed to be the Democratic Party nominee. In other words, in the party that promotes itself as the champions of the small and voiceless, it is nearly impossible for the will of the small and voiceless to supersede that of the controlling political machine. Couple that with the fact that in both parties it is practically preordained who the candidates are well in advance of any primary vote, and the actual likelihood of a Nationalist or Populist voice coming through the Democratic Party is non-existent.

This is not a conspiracy theory; in a recent interview, the chair of the Democratic National Committee Debbie Wasserman Schultz said as much in noting that "Unpledged delegates exist really to make sure that party leaders and elected officials don't have to be in a position where they are running against grass-roots activists."

God forbid that could ever occur. Who are these evil grass-roots activists? They are voters and common people. They are the very backbone of society that have entrusted the running of this nation to sanctimonious soulless cretins like Debbie Wasserman

Schultz. People truly reap what they sown when empty heads that are sent to Washington produce such empty results.

The Republican's primary process does not currently allocate delegates in this manner. At least they haven't done so yet. I would be fairly sure that going forward, they will adapt some semblance of the same system given the rise of insurgent candidates like Donald Trump and Senator Ted Cruz, people the Establishment sees as undesirable and unworthy. Republicans are simply a little slow to adapt, slow to evolve or simply incompetent on purpose. With this bunch it is sometimes hard to tell. These are the same fools that served up for sacrifice a man that couldn't remember how many houses he owned in John McCain in 2008. And they served up Mitt Romney with his binders full of women and open contempt for a full 47% of the population in 2012. This year they have thrown ~~Scott Walker, Jeb Bush, Marco~~

~~Rubio,~~ against the wall without anything sticking.

Undaunted by failure, the Republicans still do it the old fashioned way. Political insiders handpick the candidates that run for President from a shallow gene pool of smiling faces with exquisite pedigrees that curtsy to the Master Party. They choose whichever puppet that cross-eyed pollsters see as most likely to win or they promote whichever dimwit whose time had finally arrived after faithful years of disreputable service to the cause. To some extent, this process was bravely challenged by Ronald Reagan in 1976 and again in 1980, but the end results in this case were certainly palatable to the power brokers. They were, to their surprise, extraordinarily prosperous under Reagan; otherwise they would have nuked the whole damn system then.

The real alarm sounded with the campaign of Ron Paul in 2008 and 2012 and should have been a warning to the GOP Establishment that a real grass-roots movement could push a non-traditional candidate toward the destruction of their fiefdom. Of course, Ron Paul was not Donald Trump. He was not a charismatic billionaire with gobs of prior television and media exposure. Outside of the Libertarian ranks, Ron Paul was relatively obscure. Nonetheless, he spoke a Populist/Libertarian message that was not parroted by the mainstream Republican faithful and a fair share of people actually listened. It is undeniable that his message and his fortitude at charging the smart-set windmill laid the groundwork, and provided the blueprint for, the current insurgency fronted by Trump and to some degree by Ted Cruz.

I don't believe that the political establishment's angst is purely directed at the actual man that is Donald Trump. They know this guy. He has wined and dined with them and fundraised with them and contributed to various campaigns on both the Republican and Democratic side. Let's be honest, it would be nearly impossible to conduct billions of dollars of business in New York or Nevada without contributing in some way to the politicians that pull the strings in those states. Not doing so out of some unmovable adherence to principle would be fruitless and ultimately moronic.

Yet still, there are certainly some unknown qualities that make more than a few fat cats nervous about Trump's potential ascension to the highest office. With all prior candidates, there were various degrees of control over them through party pressure, lobbyist-driven campaign funding and who-knows-what damaging private information that could be leaked at any given moment. With Trump, there is simply less controllability and that creates nausea in the Republican political rank and file. He is not a dyed-in-the-wool Republican, so he is insulated from some of the usual party pressures. He didn't wait until it was his time. He just did it, without permission and without kissing the GOP Establishment's ring. With his vast personal wealth he is significantly less controlled by the powerful few kingmakers and by the ever-present lobbying groups with their millions of dollars flashing about. And whatever skeletons that are in his walk-in closet have either already been displayed and yawned upon, or simply not vetted yet for some unknown reason, or surprisingly not in existence. So the man himself is a problem, but any single man, no matter how rich and powerful, can still be handled to some degree. Even a Constitutionalist like Ted Cruz, someone that has honorably stood fast against the Establishment on a number of occasions, can be eventually controlled. How much money would it take to bend principles if it meant complete and total financial security for the next three generations of any given family? Even the most well-meaning and best principled have enormous temptations to refuse when they sit in Congress or in the Oval Office and almost everyone has a price.

Why then would the Establishment elitists be so willing to scorch and burn the whole damn thing to the ground if necessary? *Self preservation* is the answer and sadly they really only have themselves to blame for this predicament. It started with the not-so-expert analysis that was performed by the party when Mittens was defeated in 2012. After that trouncing, the Republicans realized there were simply not enough rich old white men left in America to win a national election. So they donned a welding mask and performed an autopsy on the party in the dark using a chain saw. They had a sudden epiphany that then needed to diversify. They needed more Hispanics, and they needed more African-Americans, and they needed more women and more Hispanic African-American women of Hindu ancestry. They needed to widen the base of the party so they marched every minority elected Republican they could muster into the national spotlight. Look everyone, here's Marco Rubio. Hello American, let us introduce you to Nikki Haley. They were certain this forceful show of inclusion would bring thousands of minorities to the Republican ranks. And as usual, they were wrong because it looked contrived. It wasn't seen by anyone as something genuine or organic.

Then they begged their existing depressed electorate to give them control of the Congress, and the people responded. The voters gave them a great majority in the House in 2012 and gave them the Senate in 2014. The numbers were there to fight, to represent, but nothing changed. In fact, it got *worse* as the Congress walked hand-in-hand with the President, forgetting all the while every promise made to achieve those majorities. That new singular government entity simply meandered forward without much more than a whimper from the newly minted Republican Congressional majority. Somewhere along the way, the Republicans basically lost the will to fight or more likely they simply figured that if you can't beat them, join them. Especially when fortunes are to be made.

The scorned voting public stood and watched with furrowed brows. They complained a little publically and some called into Rush Limbaugh's program more vociferous and foaming at the mouth. And even more did something incredibly profound and unheard of to this point. They quietly remembered.

The Establishment fears something far more intensely than Donald Trump. In reality, Donald Trump is a flawed and imperfect messenger with a flawless and nearly-perfect message. Those that quietly remembered; those 60-plus percent that felt betrayed by their own political party, now had a big alpha-male, self-funded, world famous mouthpiece. They now had someone that spoke like them and thought like them. They saw someone outside of the system and someone that hadn't broken every promise made to them. As a result, the party base widened far more as a result of Trump than any so-called expert could ever plan for with minority politicians and hackneyed research studies. The party now had millions of working poor, disenfranchised Democrats, and union members crossing over to vote for a Republican. Millions of new Republicans, some voting for the first time in their lives because they finally had enough, were energized and ready to roll into November. But there was one problem.

Inspiration can sometimes come from the strangest of places. I remember a quote from *Batman Begins* that illustrates this point best. Bruce Wayne was speaking to Alfred Pennyworth and noted that there are things that are able to exert far greater influence than just a single man. He said "As a man, I'm flesh and blood, I can be ignored, I can be destroyed; but as a symbol... as a symbol I can be incorruptible, I can be everlasting."

And therein lies the Establishment's problem: not Donald Trump but the Movement. The problem is the millions of new Republicans are not THEIR Republicans. These new Republicans are like Trump; flawed and a little imperfect and purely American.

The party elite gaze out their floor-to-ceiling windows and see the new masses of blue-collar everymen and strange new faces that steadfastly show up at polling stations to vote for a Republican. All this despite their very intellect being coarsely being disparaged by Republicans. The kingmakers gawk at the millions and they just want these people to get off their damn lawns.

Yes, they fear Trump's larger-than-life persona and occasional cringe-worthy diatribes . They fear that much less than the presence of millions of people that have finally risen from a purposefully-induced political coma. They don't fear a single extremely rich non-politician as much as they do the masses of less fortunate *voting* non-politicians that have found said person to be an unlikely symbol to rally around. They understand that as a man; as a man of 70 years, Trump can be destroyed and Father Time will do so if not some unnatural event before. But the symbol, the message, the sheer consolidation of not anger and fear but enlightenment and reason, is incorruptible.

These are the masses of people that neither call themselves Republicans nor Democrats, but would rather refer to themselves simply as Americans. And they are pissed and they have become aware. And they are voting and talking and becoming involved. They are blogging and Tweeting and listening to the airwaves and waiting on the line to express their own less than politically-correct message. They are gathering in masses and they are not backing down from propaganda, or falsehoods, or planned protests, or disparagement, or insults to their intellect. They have not walked away and they are growing in numbers exponentially. They are emboldened by an imperfect man, and driven by a belief that there is still some piece of a long lost America that can be salvaged and they are made strong by an understanding that this is likely the last chance to save the American Republic.

For far too long these true Americans have been wounded by the representation of weak men and women with canned answers, absence of morals, and by willful unaccountability. Worse yet, they have been stabbed in the back by spineless slime whose time for extinction has long been past . A wounded animal is a dangerous animal and this electorate is without a doubt the most dangerous of animals. That, girls and boys, is the greatest threat to a government that in and of itself has become neo-Fascist.

The Washington elite saunter out to the lectern in their tailored suits and two-hundred dollar ties, look down their noses at everyone and proceed to tell the people how to live their lives and how to vote. They are too blind, too arrogant and too afraid of losing power that they are unable to see that over 80% of the people want change and they want it from someone that is not beholden to the party machine. Instead, these political simpletons insult their very own electorate by lecturing how stupid and dangerous it is for the people to dare vote for someone outside their circle. The elitist have always considered themselves special, untouchable and perpetual But even sacred cows can produce dog meat when properly butchered. We just simply need to ensure the knives remain sharp.

Here is my unsolicited and unpaid advice to all the so-called experts that think we are wrong or that we are the problem. Please take your anti-Fascism rallies, and the tired flabby rhetoric and your prepackaged microwaveable figureheads and move on. If you put down your personal electronic device and if you allowed yourself a moment to step outside the safe zone that you have created for your own supposed comfort , you would see that behind the commercially produced protest signs are people that are marching against an enemy that doesn't exist. The only Fascism today is practiced by the monumental beasts that are inside the beltway, in the halls of Congress, on 1600 Pennsylvania Avenue, on the Supreme Court and in the cold corridors of the powerfully connected. The sad revolution that gave rise to their pitiful existence was accomplished years ago without as much as a whisper of dissention and without a single shot fired. We all just simply *allowed* it to happen.

But hope and knowledge are powerful kinfolk. We have hope in knowing that in the history of this great nation, the people have always endured. We endured the impossible odds of defying England in 1776 and we conquered the struggles within to create life, liberty and the pursuit of happiness for all. We endured the stain of slavery and healed together after brother killed brother, after countryman fought countryman, after the darkness of the Civil War ceded to a new sunrise over one nation united again. We saw our young die in Europe and die in the Pacific to stop the spread of genocidal tyranny and to ensure that freedom prevailed. Every so often, generations are called on to do the extraordinary. We are now being called.

Great leaders in such times are remembered. They are often revered and celebrated and monuments are built for such heroes. But they are singular in nature, confined by the limitation of being but one human being. It always has been the people in those moments that made the real difference. It is the people that unite and suffer and die and ultimately prevail. Knowing that we are right and they are wrong has given us this singular moment to give life back to the American Republic. We must stand as one, in voice and in action, to make this country something we are proud to call ours. No one person can do this for us. A single person is only flesh and blood. We, though, have become much more. We have started a New Revolution and for the first time in generations, **we are no longer ignored.** It is now up to us to make this moment the one that makes America everlasting.

"Take a bow for the new revolution. Smile and grin at the change all around. Pick up my guitar and play, just like yesterday. Then I'll get on my knees and pray we don't get fooled again." *Won't Get Fooled Again*, The Who, English rock band, 1971

www.newrevolution2016.com